Judgment Detox
JOURNAL

A Guided Exploration to Release
the Beliefs That Hold You Back
from Living a Better Life

Gabrielle Bernstein

NORTH STAR WAY

New York   London   Toronto   Sydney   New Delhi

NORTH
STAR WAY

North Star Way
An Imprint of Simon & Schuster, Inc.
1230 Avenue of the Americas
New York, NY 10020

First North Star Way hardcover edition January 2018

NORTH STAR WAY and colophon are trademarks of Simon & Schuster, Inc.

For information about special discounts for bulk purchases, please contact Simon & Schuster Special Sales at 1-866-506-1949 or business@simonandschuster.com.

The North Star Way Speakers Bureau can bring authors to your live event. For more information or to book an event, contact the North Star Way Speakers Bureau at 1-212-698-8888 or visit our website at www.thenorthstarway.com.

Interior design by Tracey Edelstein.
Cover design by Micaela Ezra.

Manufactured in the United States of America

10 9 8 7 6 5 4 3 2 1

Library of Congress Cataloging-in-Publication Data is available.

ISBN 978-1-5011-8467-3

Judgment Detox
JOURNAL

Welcome to the _Judgment Detox Journal!_ Opening this journal means that you're ready to release the beliefs that hold you back from living a better life.

To begin the journey of healing judgment and restoring love, we must recognize that we all have the same problem and the same solution. Our problem is that we separated from love and the solution is to return to love.

In my book <u>Judgment Detox</u> I share an interactive six-step process that calls on spiritual principles that are easy to commit to and apply in your daily life. Each lesson builds upon the next to support true healing. When you follow the process and become willing to let go, judgment, pain, and suffering will begin to dissolve. You will use this journal for each step and to practice the exercises listed. This journal is designed specifically for you to celebrate the miracles and document your process every step of the way.

Let's get started!

The way out of *judgment* begins when you witness the *judgment* without more *judgment*.

*When we take an
honest inventory of
the ways we judge,
we can become aware
of the root cause
of all our suffering:*
the separation from love.

STEP 1:
WITNESS YOUR JUDGMENT WITHOUT JUDGMENT

The process of witnessing our darkness is a brave and sacred act of love. Being willing to accept the parts of our consciousness that are out of spiritual alignment makes us stronger.

This prayer is an opening that will help you surrender to the spiritual steps laid out before you. Allow it to guide you to commit to your desire to be free and to begin Step 1.

LET'S PRAY:

I thank my higher self, the voice of love and wisdom within me. Thank you for granting me the willingness to open this book and begin this journey. I am willing to be free. I am willing to be happy. I am willing to witness my judgment without judgment.

Now you're energetically prepared to look at your judgment.

Rewrite the following phrase below:

I am willing to witness my judgment without judgment.

I am willing to witness my judgment without judgment.

_____

_____

_____

_____

_____

_____

_____

_____

_____

_____

_____

Fill out the sections below to begin the process of witnessing your judgment.

1. What or whom am I judging?
_____

2. How does this judgment make me feel?
_____

3. Why do I feel justified in this judgment?
_____

4. What moment in my life triggered me to feel justified in this judgment?
_____

1. What or whom am I judging?
_____

2. How does this judgment make me feel?
_____

3. Why do I feel justified in this judgment?
_____

4. What moment in my life triggered me to
feel justified in this judgment?
_____

1. What or whom am I judging?

_____

2. How does this judgment make me feel?

_____

3. Why do I feel justified in this judgment?

_____

4. What moment in my life triggered me to
feel justified in this judgment?

_____

1. What or whom am I judging?

2. How does this judgment make me feel?

3. Why do I feel justified in this judgment?

4. What moment in my life triggered me to
feel justified in this judgment?

1. What or whom am I judging?

_____

2. How does this judgment make me feel?

_____

3. Why do I feel justified in this judgment?

_____

4. What moment in my life triggered me to feel justified in this judgment?

_____

1. What or whom am I judging?

_____

2. How does this judgment make me feel?

_____

3. Why do I feel justified in this judgment?

_____

4. What moment in my life triggered me to
feel justified in this judgment?

_____

1. What or whom am I judging?

_____

2. How does this judgment make me feel?

_____

3. Why do I feel justified in this judgment?

_____

4. What moment in my life triggered me to
feel justified in this judgment?

_____

1. What or whom am I judging?

_____

2. How does this judgment make me feel?

_____

3. Why do I feel justified in this judgment?

_____

4. What moment in my life triggered me to
feel justified in this judgment?

_____

Once you complete the four sections, take some time to reflect on what you've uncovered. Answer the following questions:

Are there any patterns in your judgment?

_____

_____

_____

_____

_____

_____

_____

_____

_____

_____

_____

_____

Did anything you uncovered
surprise you?

_____

_____

_____

_____

_____

_____

_____

_____

_____

_____

_____

_____

_____

_____

How does it make you feel
to witness your judgment?

_____

_____

_____

_____

_____

_____

_____

_____

_____

_____

_____

_____

_____

_____

Did you judge yourself for
your own judgment?

_____

_____

_____

_____

_____

_____

_____

_____

_____

_____

_____

_____

_____

Did it bring you relief to look at the judgment?

_____

_____

_____

_____

_____

_____

_____

_____

_____

_____

_____

_____

_____

_____

Did it make you uncomfortable to look at the judgment?

_____

_____

_____

_____

_____

_____

_____

_____

_____

_____

_____

_____

_____

_____

CELEBRATE
THE
Miracles

It's time to celebrate the miracle moments. A miracle moment can be as simple as having the willingness to witness your judgment throughout the day. Document your progress here.

PROJECTING our JUDGMENT ONTO OTHER PEOPLE Gives us only a TEMPORARY and TENUOUS Reprieve

STEP 2:
HONOR THE WOUND

Underneath every judgment is a core wound. Even the most minor and seemingly insignificant judgments stem from our own shame and shadows. If we don't honor the wounds and energetic patterns that dwell beneath our judgment, they will keep coming up—over and over and over again.

Throughout this step in the Judgment Detox I will guide you to use tapping to help you heal the energetic disturbances, feelings, resentments, and traumas that dwell beneath your judgmental patterns. Remember, the reason you judge is because you're avoiding an emotion that you don't want to feel. Once you begin to tap on the underlying wound, you will release the energetic disruption in your body and will feel emotionally free. In that space of emotional freedom, you'll no longer need to judge others or yourself.

TAPPING POINTS

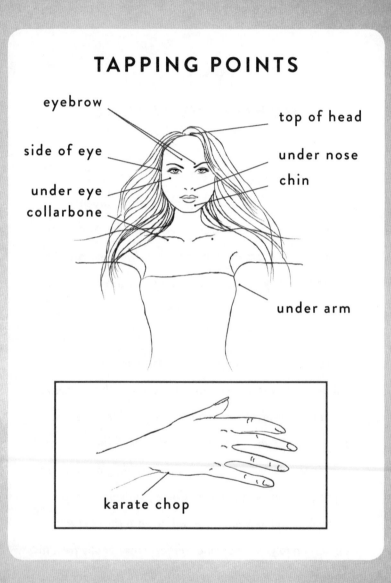

eyebrow

top of head

side of eye

under nose

chin

under eye
collarbone

under arm

karate chop

EMOTIONAL FREEDOM TECHNIQUE (EFT)

is a psychological acupressure technique that supports your emotional health. The EFT practice is simple. Follow my guidance starting on page 61 of *Judgment Detox* and stay open to receive healing.

TAPPING FOR JUDGMENT

Your MPI rating before you tap: _____

Your MPI rating after you tap: _____

Reflect for a moment on the brave step you've taken. Take five minutes to free-write about how you feel after tapping through your judgment.

_____

_____

_____

_____

_____

_____

_____

_____

_____

TAPPING FOR
FEELING JUDGED

Your MPI rating before you tap: _____

Your MPI rating after you tap: _____

Reflect for a moment on the brave step you've taken.
Take five minutes to free-write about how you feel
after tapping through your feelings of being judged.

_____

_____

_____

_____

_____

_____

_____

_____

TAPPING FOR SHAME

Your MPI rating before you tap: _____

Your MPI rating after you tap: _____

Reflect for a moment on the brave step you've taken. Take five minutes to free-write about how you feel after tapping through your shame.

_____

_____

_____

_____

_____

_____

_____

_____

_____

_____

To enhance your experience of EFT practice, tap at least once a day for thirty days. You can reference your list of judgments from Step 1 and tap on a new judgment each day for thirty days.

If new judgments come up, just add them to the list. It doesn't matter how big or small the issue is, just tap on it. The moment you witness a judgment, practice Step 1 to become more aware of the pattern of unconscious feelings underneath the judgment.

Then practice Step 2: Tap on it. At the end of the day, after you've tapped, take five minutes to write about how you feel.

TAPPING FOR:

Your MPI rating before you tap: _____

Your MPI rating after you tap: _____

_____

_____

_____

_____

_____

_____

_____

_____

_____

_____

TAPPING FOR:

Your MPI rating before you tap: _____

Your MPI rating after you tap: _____

_____

_____

_____

_____

_____

_____

_____

_____

_____

_____

_____

TAPPING FOR:

Your MPI rating before you tap: _____

Your MPI rating after you tap: _____

_____

_____

_____

_____

_____

_____

_____

_____

_____

_____

_____

_____

TAPPING FOR:

Your MPI rating before you tap: _____

Your MPI rating after you tap: _____

_____

_____

_____

_____

_____

_____

_____

_____

_____

_____

_____

_____

TAPPING FOR:

Your MPI rating before you tap: _____

Your MPI rating after you tap: _____

_____

_____

_____

_____

_____

_____

_____

_____

_____

_____

_____

TAPPING FOR:

Your MPI rating before you tap: _____

Your MPI rating after you tap: _____

_____

_____

_____

_____

_____

_____

_____

_____

_____

_____

_____

_____

TAPPING FOR:

Your MPI rating before you tap: _____

Your MPI rating after you tap: _____

_____

_____

_____

_____

_____

_____

_____

_____

_____

_____

_____

_____

TAPPING FOR:

Your MPI rating before you tap: _____

Your MPI rating after you tap: _____

_____

_____

_____

_____

_____

_____

_____

_____

_____

_____

_____

TAPPING FOR:

Your MPI rating before you tap: _____

Your MPI rating after you tap: _____

_____

_____

_____

_____

_____

_____

_____

_____

_____

_____

_____

_____

TAPPING FOR:

Your MPI rating before you tap: _____

Your MPI rating after you tap: _____

_____

_____

_____

_____

_____

_____

_____

_____

_____

_____

_____

_____

TAPPING FOR:

Your MPI rating before you tap: _____

Your MPI rating after you tap: _____

_____

_____

_____

_____

_____

_____

_____

_____

_____

_____

_____

TAPPING FOR:

Your MPI rating before you tap: _____

Your MPI rating after you tap: _____

_____

_____

_____

_____

_____

_____

_____

_____

_____

_____

_____

TAPPING FOR:

Your MPI rating before you tap: _____

Your MPI rating after you tap: _____

_____

_____

_____

_____

_____

_____

_____

_____

_____

_____

_____

_____

TAPPING FOR:

Your MPI rating before you tap: _____

Your MPI rating after you tap: _____

_____

_____

_____

_____

_____

_____

_____

_____

_____

_____

_____

_____

TAPPING FOR:

Your MPI rating before you tap: _____

Your MPI rating after you tap: _____

_____

_____

_____

_____

_____

_____

_____

_____

_____

_____

_____

TAPPING FOR:

Your MPI rating before you tap: _____

Your MPI rating after you tap: _____

_____

_____

_____

_____

_____

_____

_____

_____

_____

_____

_____

TAPPING FOR:

Your MPI rating before you tap: _____

Your MPI rating after you tap: _____

_____

_____

_____

_____

_____

_____

_____

_____

_____

_____

_____

TAPPING FOR:

Your MPI rating before you tap: _____

Your MPI rating after you tap: _____

_____

_____

_____

_____

_____

_____

_____

_____

_____

_____

_____

TAPPING FOR:

Your MPI rating before you tap: _____

Your MPI rating after you tap: _____

_____

_____

_____

_____

_____

_____

_____

_____

_____

_____

_____

TAPPING FOR:

Your MPI rating before you tap: _____

Your MPI rating after you tap: _____

_____

_____

_____

_____

_____

_____

_____

_____

_____

_____

_____

TAPPING FOR:

Your MPI rating before you tap: _____

Your MPI rating after you tap: _____

_____

_____

_____

_____

_____

_____

_____

_____

_____

_____

_____

TAPPING FOR:

Your MPI rating before you tap: _____

Your MPI rating after you tap: _____

_____

_____

_____

_____

_____

_____

_____

_____

_____

_____

_____

TAPPING FOR:

Your MPI rating before you tap: _____

Your MPI rating after you tap: _____

_____

_____

_____

_____

_____

_____

_____

_____

_____

_____

_____

_____

TAPPING FOR:

Your MPI rating before you tap: _____

Your MPI rating after you tap: _____

_____

_____

_____

_____

_____

_____

_____

_____

_____

_____

_____

_____

_____

TAPPING FOR:

Your MPI rating before you tap: _____

Your MPI rating after you tap: _____

_____

_____

_____

_____

_____

_____

_____

_____

_____

_____

_____

TAPPING FOR:

Your MPI rating before you tap: _____

Your MPI rating after you tap: _____

_____

_____

_____

_____

_____

_____

_____

_____

_____

_____

_____

TAPPING FOR:

Your MPI rating before you tap: _____

Your MPI rating after you tap: _____

_____

_____

_____

_____

_____

_____

_____

_____

_____

_____

_____

TAPPING FOR:

Your MPI rating before you tap: _____

Your MPI rating after you tap: _____

_____

_____

_____

_____

_____

_____

_____

_____

_____

_____

_____

TRUST and SURRENDER

TO EACH STEP AHEAD AND KNOW
YOU'RE BEING GUIDED.
THIS PATH IS PERFECTLY DESIGNED
FOR LONG-LASTING RELIEF
AND HAPPINESS.

CELEBRATE
THE
miracles

You've done amazing work thus far. Take a moment to celebrate the miracles and witness the distance you've already come. It takes bravery, willingness, and a deep desire to give up judgment. Be proud of yourself!

We all have
a higher power
working on our behalf
to restore our thoughts to

LOVE

STEP 3:
PUT LOVE ON THE ALTAR

In any given moment we can put love back on the altar

and let it shine through any situation or grievance.

Love can dissolve even the most deep-rooted judgment.

Now it's time to take the judgment off the altar and replace it with love. The profound act of surrendering your fear and judgment to the care of your inner guide will change the way you live. When you come to accept that you can transcend negativity whenever you choose, you'll begin to know a new form of freedom and happiness. When you pray, you begin a dialogue with the nonphysical support that is always available to you. But you cannot access this guidance without inviting it in, so when you pray, you invite the presence of love into your consciousness. To help you establish a prayer practice of your own, I've offered some of my favorite prayers. You may find that one prayer in particular resonates with you.

A PRAYER FOR SURRENDER

Releasing judgment requires spiritual surrender. Without your sincere desire to let go, you'll struggle to give over your judgment and invite in spirit. Spiritual guidance is available to you all the time. You just need to turn over your judgment to receive it. This prayer will help you align with spirit and surrender your judgment. It is a simple and powerful prayer to begin your practice of communicating with your inner guide.

LET'S PRAY:

> *Dear inner guide, I need help with my judgment toward _____. I'm ready to surrender this now. I welcome in the presence of love to guide me back to truth and grace. I'm ready to release this judgment and see through the eyes of love.*

This prayer is perfect if you're feeling stuck and resistant toward releasing your judgment. Use the surrender prayer to enter a new energetic state that supports your desire to be free from attack thoughts. This is a practice in letting go and allowing.

Take a moment to reflect on the prayer. Free-write about what you feel in the moment.

_____

_____

_____

_____

_____

_____

_____

_____

_____

_____

_____

_____

_____

_____

A PRAYER FOR ACCEPTANCE

In the Twelve Steps of Alcoholics Anonymous they say that carrying a resentment is like taking a bat and hitting yourself over the head with it. Take that in and think about how your judgment makes you feel. Maybe you feel high and justified for a few minutes, but that self-righteous satisfaction wears off. In fact, judgment lowers your energy, keeping you stuck in a low vibe. This prayer will help you accept that your judgment no longer serves you.

The acceptance prayer has helped me see through the lens of love whenever fear has me in a headlock, and I turn to this prayer whenever my judgment has gotten the best of me. I trust that it will always remind me that what I'm judging is not what I think it is. Through the energy of acceptance I release my grievances and accept a solution of the highest good. Enjoy this acceptance prayer from the Big Book of Alcoholics Anonymous:

LET'S PRAY:

Acceptance is the answer to all my problems today. When I am disturbed, it is because I find some person, place, thing, or situation—some fact of my life— unacceptable to me, and I can find no serenity until I accept that person, place, thing, or situation as being exactly the way it is supposed to be at this moment.

This prayer has a powerful energy behind it. Even if acceptance feels way out of reach, simply saying the words of this prayer will change your attitude. Practice this prayer regularly and pay attention to your internal shifts.

Take a moment to reflect on the prayer. Free-write about what you feel in the moment.

_____

_____

_____

_____

_____

_____

_____

_____

_____

_____

_____

_____

_____

_____

_____

A PRAYER TO CHOOSE AGAIN

Lesson 243 of *A Course in Miracles* offers this affirmation: "Today I will judge nothing that occurs." I use this message from the *Course* as a daily prayer to help me choose to release my judgment. This prayer is a powerful way to begin your day: Judgment is a choice you make, and when you align your mind with the choice to release judgment you will be guided to do so. Practice using this prayer in the morning when you wake up. The moment you open your eyes, recite, "Today I will judge nothing that occurs." Pay close attention to how the rest of your day flows. You may be quicker to catch yourself in a judgmental thought or you may stop yourself from saying something judgmental and choose another topic instead.

LET'S PRAY:

Today I will judge nothing
that occurs.

These seven words are simple but profound. When you say this prayer you consciously choose to realign your thoughts with love and let the voice of your inner guide lead the way. The more you make this choice the less you will judge. In time this prayer will become second nature; it will be an easy solution to all your judgments. I love this practice because it keeps me committed.

If this prayer resonates with you, then set it as an alarm to go off on your phone throughout the day, and trust that spirit will intervene to restore your thoughts back to love.

Take a moment to reflect on the prayer. Free-write about what you feel in the moment.

_____

_____

_____

_____

_____

_____

_____

_____

_____

_____

_____

_____

_____

_____

_____

A PRAYER TO FORGIVE YOUR THOUGHTS

The final prayer is to forgive the thought. Whenever we have a judgmental thought, we can easily erase it through forgiveness. I've gotten into the practice of witnessing my judgmental thoughts and quickly forgiving them. I silently say to myself:

LET'S PRAY:

*I forgive this thought and I
choose again.*

This prayer offers me immediate relief. In an instant I can end the judgment cycle through the power of my intentions. When I intend to forgive the thought, I pardon myself for choosing wrongly and I realign with my right mind. In any moment I can find forgiveness through my practice. The moment you choose to forgive your thought, you realign with love and forgiveness is bestowed upon you.

Forgiveness is a practice because it is ongoing. I find that I have to forgive my thoughts throughout the day. The ego voice of judgment is always at the forefront of our minds, so we have to lean on forgiveness to reprogram our thinking and restore our thoughts back to love.

Throughout the day pay close attention to your judgments and use the prayer practice of forgiving a thought to bring you back to grace. You can do it silently anywhere, anytime. All you have to do is choose for it.

Take a moment to reflect on the prayer. Free-write about what you feel in the moment.

_____

_____

_____

_____

_____

_____

_____

_____

_____

_____

_____

_____

_____

_____

_____

_____

When you begin your prayer practice, pay attention to how you receive communication from spirit. You may have past experiences of receiving guidance that you can now lean on to help develop your faith. Take a moment to think about any times in your life where you've received nonphysical guidance and write those examples here.

_____

_____

_____

_____

_____

_____

_____

_____

_____

_____

_____

CELEBRATE
THE
Miracles

Remember that this is a process and celebrate the miracles along the way by documenting them here. There is no need to aim for a major breakthrough. Add up each miracle moment, and when you're done, you'll look back and be amazed by the shifts.

When we put aside
our stories, pretense,
and judgment,

can be restored.

STEP 4:
SEE FOR THE FIRST TIME

Seeing others for the first time means we see their innocence and oneness. We can recognize the light within them as the same light that shines within ourselves. In the presence of someone's light, judgment cannot live.

EXERCISE IN ACCEPTANCE

Begin your practice of acceptance by revisiting your list of judgments from Step 1. Pick one from the list that is still triggering you, even after the EFT and prayer. Maybe you're afraid to release a judgment toward a person who's harmed you or maybe you're afraid of what will happen if you stop judging yourself. Choose a judgment that you're ready to release and bring it to your practice now.

At the top of the next page, write the name of the person you've judged. (Maybe it's your own name!)

Next, write a list of all the aspects about this person that you like.

NAME:

Positive Aspects

* _____
* _____
* _____
* _____
* _____
* _____
* _____
* _____
* _____
* _____
* _____
* _____
* _____
* _____

NAME:

Positive Aspects

* _____
* _____
* _____
* _____
* _____
* _____
* _____
* _____
* _____
* _____
* _____
* _____
* _____

NAME:

Positive Aspects

* _____
* _____
* _____
* _____
* _____
* _____
* _____
* _____
* _____
* _____
* _____
* _____
* _____

NAME:

Positive Aspects

* _____
* _____
* _____
* _____
* _____
* _____
* _____
* _____
* _____
* _____
* _____
* _____
* _____
* _____

NAME:

Positive Aspects

* _____
* _____
* _____
* _____
* _____
* _____
* _____
* _____
* _____
* _____
* _____
* _____
* _____
* _____

NAME:

Positive Aspects

* _____
* _____
* _____
* _____
* _____
* _____
* _____
* _____
* _____
* _____
* _____
* _____
* _____
* _____

NAME:

Positive Aspects

* _____
* _____
* _____
* _____
* _____
* _____
* _____
* _____
* _____
* _____
* _____
* _____
* _____
* _____

NAME:

Positive Aspects

* _____
* _____
* _____
* _____
* _____
* _____
* _____
* _____
* _____
* _____
* _____
* _____
* _____
* _____

NAME:

Positive Aspects

* _____
* _____
* _____
* _____
* _____
* _____
* _____
* _____
* _____
* _____
* _____
* _____
* _____
* _____

NAME:

Positive Aspects

* _____
* _____
* _____
* _____
* _____
* _____
* _____
* _____
* _____
* _____
* _____
* _____
* _____
* _____

NAME:

Positive Aspects

* _____
* _____
* _____
* _____
* _____
* _____
* _____
* _____
* _____
* _____
* _____
* _____
* _____

NAME:

Positive Aspects

* _____
* _____
* _____
* _____
* _____
* _____
* _____
* _____
* _____
* _____
* _____
* _____
* _____
* _____

NAME:

Positive Aspects

* _____
* _____
* _____
* _____
* _____
* _____
* _____
* _____
* _____
* _____
* _____
* _____
* _____
* _____

NAME:

Positive Aspects

* _____
* _____
* _____
* _____
* _____
* _____
* _____
* _____
* _____
* _____
* _____
* _____
* _____
* _____

NAME:

Positive Aspects

* _____
* _____
* _____
* _____
* _____
* _____
* _____
* _____
* _____
* _____
* _____
* _____
* _____
* _____

NAME:

Positive Aspects

* _____
* _____
* _____
* _____
* _____
* _____
* _____
* _____
* _____
* _____
* _____
* _____
* _____
* _____

NAME:

Positive Aspects

* _____
* _____
* _____
* _____
* _____
* _____
* _____
* _____
* _____
* _____
* _____
* _____
* _____
* _____

NAME:

Positive Aspects

* _____
* _____
* _____
* _____
* _____
* _____
* _____
* _____
* _____
* _____
* _____
* _____
* _____
* _____

NAME:

Positive Aspects

* _____
* _____
* _____
* _____
* _____
* _____
* _____
* _____
* _____
* _____
* _____
* _____
* _____
* _____

NAME:

Positive Aspects

* _____

* _____

* _____

* _____

* _____

* _____

* _____

* _____

* _____

* _____

* _____

* _____

* _____

* _____

Compassion is the antidote to judgment. When you accept someone right where they are, you can see them for all their good *and* bad. Cultivating a perception of compassion helps you see someone's innocence. Seeing them with compassion helps you see their hardship, pain, and deep suffering.

Take the next few pages and cultivate a compassion list. Write down any wrongdoings you've encountered and focus on what might have allowed that person to behave in such a fashion. When you redirect your focus away from what has been done and onto the sickness that led someone to do something, compassion can set in.

CELEBRATE
THE
miracles

Seeing others for the first time is the greatest gift you can give yourself. Ultimately you set *yourself* free. You free yourself from the imprisonment of judgment and recalibrate your energy to live in harmony with the light of the world. Celebrate your miracles now.

MEDITATION

has the capacity to

transform all your

RELATIONSHIPS

including your

relationship

to

YOURSELF

STEP 5:
CUT THE CORDS

When you tune in to the energy of love through your meditation practice, you invite an invisible force of love to take over. In the presence of that love, the past can fade away and the energetic cords of judgment can dissolve.

CORD-CUTTING MEDITATION

Following your meditation practice, take note of how it made you feel. Free-write for five minutes.

_____

_____

_____

_____

_____

_____

_____

_____

_____

_____

_____

_____

_____
_____
_____
_____
_____
_____
_____
_____
_____
_____
_____
_____
_____
_____

MEDITATION FOR FORGIVENESS

Following your meditation practice, take note of how it made you feel. Free-write for five minutes.

_____
_____
_____
_____
_____
_____
_____
_____
_____
_____
_____

Following your meditation practice, take note of how it made you feel. Free-write for five minutes.

_____

_____

_____

_____

_____

_____

_____

_____

_____

_____

_____

_____

THE MANTRA MEDITATION

Following your meditation practice, take note of how it made you feel. Free-write for five minutes.

_____

_____

_____

_____

_____

_____

_____

_____

_____

_____

_____

_____

_____

MEDITATION FOR ONENESS

Following your meditation practice, take note of how
it made you feel. Free-write for five minutes.

_____

_____

_____

_____

_____

_____

_____

_____

_____

_____

_____

_____

GREAT RAYS MEDITATION

Following your meditation practice, take note of how it made you feel. Free-write for five minutes.

_____

_____

_____

_____

_____

_____

_____

_____

_____

_____

_____

_____

CELEBRATE
THE
Miracles

Through meditation we slow down our mind and reorganize our energy, which clears space for our inner guidance system to function. The more you make meditation a daily habit, the weaker the ego's resistance will become. You'll grow to rely on meditation to feel connected to love. Let's celebrate the miracles now.

Our unwillingness to

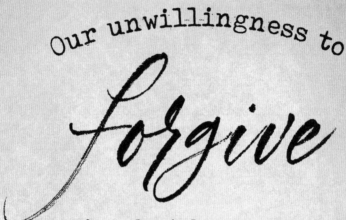

forgive

is what keeps us
in the judgment cycle.

STEP 6:
BRING YOUR SHADOWS TO LIGHT

Your willingness to forgive brings the darkness of your illusions to the light of your truth. When you decide to expose your fear to spirit for healing, you are undoing denial and judgment. When you let light shine in, you allow for true healing.

The workbook of *A Course in Miracles* says:

> *You are not trapped in the world*
> *you see, because its cause can be*
> *changed. This change requires,*
> *first, that the cause be identified*
> *and then [second] let go, so that*
> *[third] it can be replaced. The*
> *first two steps in this process*
> *require your cooperation. The*
> *final one does not.*

Put pen to paper and follow this guidance. In writing, offer your judgment over to the care of your inner guide for forgiveness.

Step 1: Whom have you judged and how does it make you feel?

_____

Step 2: Choose again and write about why you're willing to let it go.

_____

Step 3: Ask spirit to help you forgive.

_____

Step 1: Whom have you judged and
how does it make you feel?

Step 2: Choose again and write about
why you're willing to let it go.

Step 3: Ask spirit to help you forgive.

Step 1: Whom have you judged and
how does it make you feel?

_____

Step 2: Choose again and write about
why you're willing to let it go.

_____

Step 3: Ask spirit to help you forgive.

_____

Step 1: Whom have you judged and
how does it make you feel?

Step 2: Choose again and write about
why you're willing to let it go.

Step 3: Ask spirit to help you forgive.

Step 1: Whom have you judged and
how does it make you feel?

Step 2: Choose again and write about
why you're willing to let it go.

Step 3: Ask spirit to help you forgive.

Step 1: Whom have you judged and
how does it make you feel?

Step 2: Choose again and write about
why you're willing to let it go.

Step 3: Ask spirit to help you forgive.

Step 1: Whom have you judged and
how does it make you feel?

_____

Step 2: Choose again and write about
why you're willing to let it go.

_____

Step 3: Ask spirit to help you forgive.

_____

Step 1: Whom have you judged and
how does it make you feel?

Step 2: Choose again and write about
why you're willing to let it go.

Step 3: Ask spirit to help you forgive.

Step 1: Whom have you judged and
how does it make you feel?

_____

Step 2: Choose again and write about
why you're willing to let it go.

_____

Step 3: Ask spirit to help you forgive.

_____

Step 1: Whom have you judged and
how does it make you feel?

_____

Step 2: Choose again and write about
why you're willing to let it go.

_____

Step 3: Ask spirit to help you forgive.

_____

Step 1: Whom have you judged and
how does it make you feel?

_____

Step 2: Choose again and write about
why you're willing to let it go.

_____

Step 3: Ask spirit to help you forgive.

_____

Step 1: Whom have you judged and
how does it make you feel?

_____

Step 2: Choose again and write about
why you're willing to let it go.

_____

Step 3: Ask spirit to help you forgive.

_____

THE PROMISE OF FORGIVENESS

The promise of forgiveness is freedom from the bondage of judgment and attack. Forgiveness bridges your fear back to love and restores your connection to the love of the Universe. When you welcome forgiveness, you're relinquishing fear and remembering love. Forgiving eyes see only light.

Make self-forgiveness a priority by practicing the three steps of forgiveness on yourself. Take a moment to answer each question. You might be able to think of a number of ways in which you have been unforgiving toward yourself. If so, list them here and offer them up to spirit.

S T E P 1: How have you been unforgiving toward yourself, and how does it make you feel?

_____

_____

_____

_____

_____

_____

_____

_____

_____

_____

_____

_____

_____

_____

_____

_____

STEP 2: Choose again and write about why you're willing to let it go.

_____

_____

_____

_____

_____

_____

_____

_____

_____

_____

_____

_____

_____

_____

STEP 3: Ask Spirit to help you forgive.

_____

_____

_____

_____

_____

_____

_____

_____

_____

_____

_____

_____

_____

_____

CELEBRATE
THE
Miracles

Your desire for joy and freedom will keep you on your path and connected to each step. Each time your mind wanders into judgment, ask yourself, "Am I willing to be free?" This question will catapult you back into the practice and the steps will be there to lift you up. Trust this process and know you're always being guided. Let's celebrate the miracles now.

HOW
TO
Live
the
JUDGMENT DETOX

When
one person
remembers their
TRUE NATURE,
they light up
the world.

THE PROMISE

When you follow this practice, you'll no longer need to look outside yourself for happiness and self-worth. When you're aligned with the presence of love, you know you are good enough, lovable, and powerful. You remember who you truly are. That is the mission of this book. When more and more people realign with their truth, separation will end. Judgment and attack cannot coexist with love and oneness. Terror and fear cannot survive in the light of awakened beings. When people wake up on a large scale, the world as we know it will shift.

We are living in a time that requires us to wake up. It is our birthright to feel connected, and we're called to return to that truth. We must live this truth in every corner of our lives in order to heal the state of the world. This is why we're here: to go on a journey of unlearning fear and remembering love.

Gabrielle Bernstein is the #1 *New York Times* bestselling author of *The Universe Has Your Back* as well as *Miracles Now, May Cause Miracles, Add More ~ing to Your Life, Spirit Junkie,* and *Judgment Detox*. She was featured on Oprah's *SuperSoul Sunday* as a "next-generation thought leader" and the *New York Times* named her "a new role model." She appears regularly as an expert on *The Dr. Oz Show* and cohosted the Guinness World Record largest guided meditation with Deepak Chopra.